THE EIGHTY-YEAR RULE

THE EIGHTY-YEAR RULE

What Would You Regret
Not Doing in Your Lifetime?

CLAIRE YEUNG

OPEN BOOK EDITIONS
A Berrett-Koehler Partner

iUniverse®

THE EIGHTY-YEAR RULE
WHAT WOULD YOU REGRET NOT DOING IN YOUR LIFETIME?

iUniverse books may be ordered through booksellers or by contacting:

iUniverse
1663 Liberty Drive
Bloomington, IN 47403
www.iuniverse.com
1-800-Authors (1-800-288-4677)

Because of the dynamic nature of the Internet, any web addresses or links contained in this book may have changed since publication and may no longer be valid. The views expressed in this work are solely those of the author and do not necessarily reflect the views of the publisher, and the publisher hereby disclaims any responsibility for them.

Any people depicted in stock imagery provided by Thinkstock are models, and such images are being used for illustrative purposes only. Certain stock imagery © Thinkstock.

ISBN: 978-1-4917-7074-0 (sc)
ISBN: 978-1-4917-7075-7 (e)

Library of Congress Control Number: 2015909632

Print information available on the last page.

iUniverse rev. date: 07/14/2015

Whether or not you believe in reincarnation, you only have one life in your present form. Why not make every moment of this precious time count?

Dedication

This book is dedicated to my grandpa, Henry Hon Lit Siu. He was born on August 18, 1910. He was a visionary, a free spirit and a really amazing role model. He decided to leave the comfort of his life as a banker in Hong Kong in 1968 to move himself and his family to Canada because he thought that his children and grandchildren would have better opportunities in Canada. (In the late 1960s, there was a great deal of unrest in Hong Kong. As a small child, I witnessed the rioting in the streets.) After moving to Vancouver, British Columbia, he embarked on a second career as a real estate agent at the age of 60. Not bad for a guy for whom English was a second language. He became an integral part of the Chinese community, volunteering his time at the Chinese Cultural Centre and the Sun Yet Sen Gardens. He would give his bottom dollar to someone if he felt that person needed it more than he did. He hired newly immigrated Chinese people to do odd jobs around the house to help them earn some extra money. He passed away on October 31, 1997. When I think of the word *courage*, I see my grandfather. I miss him immensely. I live each and every day of my life inspired by his spirit.

Have you ever dreamed about taking a
year off work to go see the world?

Have you ever dreamed about
making a career change?

Have you ever dreamed about going back to school?

Have you ever dreamed about
starting your own business?

Have you ever dreamed about running a marathon?

Have you ever dreamed about
cycling across the country?

Have you ever dreamed about becoming a sculptor?

Have you ever dreamed about
sailing around the world?

Have you ever dreamed about doing what you love?

What's stopping you?

Contents

Introduction

The only way to live is to accept each minute as an
unrepeatable miracle, which is exactly what it is: a
miracle and unrepeatable.

—Margaret Storm Jameson

My intention with this book is to provide you with the courageous
space you need to discover your authentic self, your purpose,
your passion, which seek to emerge from within, so that you
can make the most of every moment in your life. I know you
have something unique to contribute to the world. I also know
that if each and every one of us contributed our unique gifts,
the world would be a better place.

I invite you to step into the courageous space that I'm holding
for you and take the journey toward discovering your authentic
self, embracing your purpose and creating your life's path.

Chapter One

Maybe It's a Virus

Sometimes the moments that challenge us the most define us.

—Deena Kastor

I had been an attorney for 23 years when in March 2012, while training for the Vancouver International Marathon, I got sick. All of a sudden, I couldn't run one mile, let alone 26.2. Bam! I was suddenly stopped dead in my tracks. I found that I had no energy whatsoever. I could hardly get out of bed. My doctor had me tested for everything under the sun. Maybe it was a thyroid issue; maybe it was an autoimmune disorder; maybe it was a virus. No one knew what was actually wrong with me. After six months of endless medical tests, my doctor decided I probably had some sort of virus, which was really code for "we have no idea."

Being an endurance runner made me feel strong, capable and confident. When I started experiencing health problems and lost the ability to run, all of a sudden I felt incredibly vulnerable, like I'd lost my mojo. Those six months made me reflect upon my life's purpose and why I was here on this earth. What was I doing to make the world a better place? What was my true calling? Being an attorney had never been my dream career. It was just a job where I could earn a good living. I was 50 years old and in a job that I didn't love, waiting out the next 10 years for retirement. *Wow, how the hell did I get here?*

Let me tell you my backstory to put things into context. I was born in Hong Kong in 1962. Typhoon Wanda blew through town the day after I was born. Wanda blew the roof off the hospital, forcing my mom and me to evacuate. This event was a foreshadowing of the tumultuous times ahead for Hong Kong in the 1960s.

In 1967, riots broke out in Hong Kong as a result of growing dissatisfaction with British colonial rule. What initially began as a labour dispute between trade unions and factory owners culminated in full-scale violence. Pro-Communist leftists clashed with the Hong Kong police, planting bombs throughout the city and murdering anti-leftist radio commentator Lam Bun. The violence subsided only when Premier Zhou Enlai of the People's Republic of China ordered the leftist groups in Hong Kong to stop the bombings in December 1967. As a result of the unrest and uncertainty over Hong Kong's future as a British colony, many of the residents of Hong Kong decided to immigrate to North America. I recall my grandparents and parents being concerned about communist influence on Hong Kong and whether the People's Republic of China would take back the British colony before the 1997 handover. This is what prompted my family to leave a very comfortable middle-class life in Hong Kong to start again in Canada.

In 1969, my parents and I followed my grandparents' lead, leaving Hong Kong for Canada. We landed in Vancouver, British Columbia, on April 1. When my parents told me that we were moving to Canada, I had visions of us living in a mansion with a gated entrance, a long tree-lined driveway and a pool like I'd seen in the movies. I was quite disappointed when we arrived at my grandparents' home in Vancouver, a modest three-bedroom house in a quiet neighbourhood—no gated entrance, no long tree-lined driveway and no pool. I'd also assumed that our lifestyle would be very similar to what we'd enjoyed in Hong Kong. We'd had a live-in housekeeper/cook, a live-in nanny and a driver who drove me to private school in Hong Kong. Much to my surprise, we enjoyed none of those luxuries in Canada. Not only were there no more nannies, housekeepers and cooks, but my parents and I had to live with my grandparents after we arrived in Canada because my parents had not secured employment prior to leaving Hong Kong. In my grandparents' modest home resided my parents and me, my uncle, who was in university, and my aunt and her husband, who were finishing their residency to become doctors. A full house!

Starting over in a new country meant a huge step down the socio-economic ladder for my family. In Hong Kong, my grandfather was a banker and my grandmother was an elementary-school principal. They lived in a large three-bedroom apartment in an upscale neighbourhood of Hong Kong. My grandfather owned a racehorse and belonged to the very prestigious Hong Kong Jockey Club. When my parents got married, there were 700 guests at their wedding. The threat of communist influence in Hong Kong must have been incredibly frightening for my grandparents to decide at ages 58 and 52 to leave their privileged lifestyle behind to face the unknown in a new country they'd never set foot in before.

At the time we arrived in Vancouver, my family had very few life skills in terms of day-to-day living in North America. No one knew how to mow the lawn or do yard work or housework or cook. Those were not skills that we'd needed in Hong Kong. There was a huge learning curve on the life-skills front for everyone in my family. On top of that, my parents also had to find work. In Hong Kong, my dad worked in middle management for an arm of the government, and my mom was a teacher. Fortunately, everyone in my family, except for me, spoke English fluently (one advantage of living in a British colony). But my grandfather developed quite a green thumb over the years, growing more than 100 rose bushes in our yard, as well as growing bonsai plants on the back deck.

I still remember my first day of school. My parents walked me up to the school on the Monday after we arrived in Vancouver to enrol me in Grade 1. My English vocabulary consisted of about five words. My parents had a conversation with the school principal that I couldn't understand, and the next thing I knew my parents were handing me over to the principal. They told me they would come back at lunchtime to take me home and then would walk me back to school after lunch. They wished me good luck and waved goodbye. I stood there, dumbfounded, and then started to cry. "What do you mean you're leaving me here with this stranger who speaks no Cantonese?"

The principal took me to the Grade 1 class and introduced me to the teacher. That was my first taste of my family's "sink or swim" philosophy. Until lunchtime, I was there in a classroom with non-Cantonese speaking people. I decided I might as well make the best of it and try to decipher what was going on. If nothing else, my parents and my grandparents were very pragmatic people. I would eventually have to go to school, so there was no sense delaying the inevitable. And besides, I would learn English much faster being thrown into an English-speaking environment. Of course, they were right. By the time my parents came back to fetch me at lunchtime, I'd made a few friends and was eager to go back to school after lunch.

Because both my parents worked (my dad as program manager for a non-profit, my mom a teacher at a Catholic school), we continued to live with my grandparents so that they could help to look after me. That was probably one of the best things that ever happened to me. I had the opportunity to spend a great deal of time with my grandfather, tagging along to the horse races, the bowling alley and for dim sum lunches. He taught me some really valuable life lessons: care about your community, be generous toward others, be kind to everyone and, most of all, have fun. I also benefited from my grandmother's wisdom—and her spaghetti and meat sauce, which she made for me every day after school. When I was about 10 years old, she told me that as a girl, I had to get a good education and then a good job so that I could stand on my own two feet and not have to depend on someone else to provide for me. I have never forgotten her advice.

Fast forward 40-odd years. How did I end up in a career that I wasn't passionate about, working just for the money? As the saying goes, hindsight is 20/20. Looking back at the first 50 years of my life at what I thought was the *why* behind my parents' and grandparents' decisions, I now see how totally off-base I was. I'd lived the first half of my life thinking that my life's purpose was to regain the affluent lifestyle that we'd enjoyed in Hong Kong. I believed that my parents went back to university to get their master's degrees to further their careers so that they could make more money. Yes, that was part of it, but the part that never dawned on me was that they loved their work and wanted to be the best they could be. My mom is a really accomplished woman. She was the first Chinese woman to be appointed principal of an elementary school in the Vancouver School Board; she had been a lecturer at the University of British Columbia, and she was an expert on teaching children with learning disabilities. My dad loves information. He reads the newspaper, watches the news and loves to amuse people with tidbits of miscellaneous information. He is also one of the kindest people I know.

For me, becoming an attorney was just something I sort of fell into. None of the careers available to business school graduates really interested me, so going to law school was a good way to put off "getting a real job." After law school, I ended up practicing law in the areas of human rights, labour, and employment—interesting enough but certainly not work that I had a burning passion for. The income was good, so I didn't think about whether I actually enjoyed what I was doing. I was totally focused on regaining the affluent lifestyle I knew as a child in Hong Kong. It wasn't until I was struck by my mysterious illness that I started to question the *why* behind my life's decisions.

My grandparents had the courage to start over in a new country. My parents built their careers from the ground up in a new country. My family lived by the sink-or-swim philosophy. You jump in with both feet and figure it out—no whining, no coddling, no feeling sorry for yourself and, most of all, no crying.

I took matters into my own hands in September 2012 (just after my 50th birthday). I walked away from my six-figure job as an attorney. When I was feeling like the walking dead most days, I simply could not sustain the 50- to 70-hour work-weeks that my job demanded. I decided it was time for me to put my career on the back burner and regain my health. Was it scary? Hell yes! But most of all it was like a giant weight had been lifted from my shoulders. It was incredibly liberating to simply walk away and not know what was next. No plan, no destination, just an open road. Here was my chance to figure it out. Sink or swim. I learned to adventure race at the age of 37 and ran my first marathon at the age of 48, so I chose to believe that at the age of 50 I could walk away from my job to find a more meaningful life. The only thing I knew for certain when I walked away from my job was that I wanted to do work that inspired me, that gave my life purpose and meaning, that truly helped others.

Wow, jobless at 50, with no idea what I really wanted to be when I grew up. Definitely not how I'd envisioned my life unfolding.

Chapter Two

Through the Looking Glass

Promise me you'll always remember: You're braver than you believe, and stronger than you seem, and smarter than you think.

—A.A. Milne

The funny thing about life is that there's always a flip side to every situation. On the one hand, it was liberating to walk away from a job I didn't love; on the other hand, being unemployed caused my self-esteem to take a huge nosedive. I found it hard to tell people that I was taking a break from working to regain my health and to figure out my life's purpose. Somehow, saying that out loud made it sound as if I were doing something verboten. Not having a job at the age of 50 felt shameful to me. Was I really doing the right thing by quitting a well-paying job to pursue this crazy notion of mine? Maybe there was no such thing as a true calling or true purpose to one's life.

Then I stumbled upon Brené Brown's TED Talk, *Listening to Shame*. Those 20 minutes changed my life. Hearing her say, "Vulnerability is the birthplace of innovation, creativity and change" gave me goose bumps. As she spoke about shame, our inner doubters and the fear of failure, I got shivers up my spine. When Brown recited Theodore Roosevelt's *Man in the Arena* quote, it strengthened my resolve to find my true calling:

It is not the critic who counts; not the man who points out how the strong man stumbles, or where the doer of deeds could have done them better. The credit belongs to the man who is actually in the arena, whose face is marred by dust and sweat and blood; who strives valiantly; who errs, who comes short again and again, because there is no effort without error and shortcoming; but who does actually strive to do the deeds; who knows great enthusiasms, the great devotions; who spends himself in a worthy cause; who at the best knows in the end the triumph of high achievement, and who at the worst, if he fails, at least fails while daring greatly, so that his place shall never be with those cold and timid souls who neither know victory nor defeat.

From that moment on, I knew I had to dare greatly. Sitting on the sidelines, not challenging myself to be all that I could be, not reaching my full potential, not pursuing my true calling would mean that I had squandered my life away. And that would be tragic! Brown's TED Talk helped me to reframe my perception of myself. There was nothing to be ashamed of about being unemployed at 50. It takes courage to walk away from a well-paying job to reinvent oneself and one's life.

That's what led me to become a Whole Person Certified Coach through Coach Training World in Portland. During my coaching training, it became clear to me that my life's purpose was to be the mirror for others so that they could see the possibilities in their own lives. The one big reason why I am on this earth is to see the best, the bravest, the strongest, the most successful, the most powerful parts of others and to reflect that back to them so that they too can see what I see.

From that moment on, I knew that my true calling was to help others make the most of their lives, to live boldly and without regret.

Chapter Three

The Eighty-Year Rule

I regret nothing.
—Brigitte Bardot

Whenever she's faced with a decision point in her life, my partner, Vivienne, uses the Eighty-Year Rule to decide what to do. She asks herself, "When I'm 80 years old and I look back on my life, will I regret not taking this opportunity/doing this thing?" This approach has served her well. She's had three career changes so far and has taken four sabbaticals. Vivienne worked as a member of the Royal Canadian Mounted Police, then as a shelter manager for the Society for the Prevention of Cruelty to Animals (SPCA) and then decided to go to law school to become an attorney. During her 20 years of practice as an attorney, she took time away from her career to travel Europe for six months on her motorcycle, pursue two master's degrees, teach English in China and teach international law at a law school in Russia.

Becoming a Whole Person Certified Coach was one thing. But what would I do with my coaching credentials? Would I join a consulting firm? Find a job with an organization as a corporate coach? Start up my own coaching business? I had no experience as an entrepreneur and the prospect of not having a regular paycheque seemed incredibly scary to me.

Yet, in my heart of hearts, I knew that the only way for me to help others to live boldly and without regret was to create the products and services that would allow me to do that. So, I looked to the Eighty-Year Rule for guidance. Would I regret not taking the risk of starting up my own business that would allow me to live my purpose and pursue my true calling? Put in those terms, it was clear that I had no other choice but to dare greatly. That's how my company The Peloton Group Coaching Inc. was born.

Chapter Four

Uncharted Waters

The greatest thing is at any moment, to be willing to give up who we are in order to become all that we can become.

—Max de Pree

Holy smokes! The prospect of becoming an entrepreneur was exponentially scarier than quitting my job. I knew nothing about running my own business. But I chose to believe that everything I'd learned in business school and in law school had prepared me for this moment. Those accounting, finance and tax law courses wouldn't go to waste after all!

I decided that instead of starting out by making a business plan, as any business grad or banker would advise, I would start by creating a vision board where I could define what my business means to me in terms of my purpose, my passion, my core values and my overall life's goals. My career decisions had been guided by money the first 50 years of my life. This time, I knew that my business had to be guided by my heart and my soul. Anything other than that wouldn't be worth creating.

The moment I started writing things down on the piece of poster paper, my vision for what I wanted to create became more and more clear. Articulating my core values was a no-brainer:

passion, adventure, inspiration, strength and authenticity. (No wonder my job as an attorney was a bad fit for me. There aren't too many law firms or companies out there that lead with those values.) I decided that those five core values would be non-negotiable and that they would form the foundation of my business. Defining my passion was a cinch: experiencing adventure, living life to the fullest, running and cycling. I knew that my purpose was to help others uncover their full potential so that they could live extraordinary lives. That absolutely had to be the mission of my company as well.

How did I know that I was on the right path? A couple months after I incorporated my company, I stumbled upon Scott Dinsmore's 2012 TED Golden Gate talk. He spoke about inspiring possibility and doing work that inspires you. Scott ends his talk with the question, "What is the work you can't not do?" Faced with that question, I knew, without a doubt, that I was on the right path. I just needed to figure out how to create the products and services that I wanted to offer in my coaching business.

I knew that, first of all, I would need seed money to get my coaching business off the ground. After trying out some low-cost options, such as creating my own website using a stock web hosting service, I knew that if I wanted to build a business that I could be proud of, I had to enlist expert assistance, and that wouldn't be cheap. My partner, Vivienne, and I decided that I was worth betting on, so we decided to put the money we'd saved up for our kitchen renovation toward starting up my business.

The funny thing about making a major life shift is that the people around you (friends, family, colleagues) only know you in a certain context, and some of them are not ready or able to believe that you can succeed on your new path. If I had a dollar for every person who offered me advice about the perils of embarking on a new career path at the age of 50, I would have a bucketful of dollar bills. Here are a few of my favourites:

- Aren't you a bit old to be starting up your own business?
- Being an entrepreneur is overrated.
- You know that most new businesses fail, don't you? Lots of people have great ideas, but selling them is a whole other thing. That's where people fail.

And your point is ...?

At first, people's negative comments really bothered me. Why were they raining on my parade? But one day I had an epiphany. It occurred to me that those negative comments were more a reflection of those people's limiting beliefs about their own lives rather than a statement about my journey. The moment I realized that, this visual popped into my head:

> A crystal-clear mountain stream flowing over pebbles, rocks and twigs, sometimes getting caught up in the debris for a moment, then continuing on its way. As the stream travels on its way, it momentarily gets hung up on the pebbles, rocks and twigs, but it deals with the debris and continues on. The stream never circles back to see what was in its path. The water just carries on downstream.

This stream analogy is my new go-to thought whenever I encounter a speed bump in my life's journey. Learning to let go and move forward has made a huge difference in the quality of my journey through life. I'm totally at peace with the way I show up in the world and where my journey is taking me. It allows me to focus on fulfilling my life's purpose.

A quick word about limiting beliefs ...

We all hold beliefs that we've formed through our life experiences. Our beliefs are part of the fabric of who we are. Sometimes those beliefs serve a useful purpose; other times those beliefs get in our way and prevent us from living our lives to the fullest extent.

Often you don't even realize that you hold a limiting belief. All you feel when confronted with doing something that bumps up against a limiting belief is fear or discomfort. The doubter or inner critic who lives in your head plays the limiting-belief card whenever you're faced with trying something new, different or beyond your comfort zone. The doubter is afraid of failure, rejection, being the laughingstock—on and on and on.

The limiting belief that had held me back my entire life was the belief that my life's mission was to regain the affluent lifestyle that my family enjoyed in Hong Kong. That belief prevented me from seeking my true calling. I was so blinded by my desire to achieve an affluent lifestyle that I never took the time to align my life's journey with my core values and true passions. Living a life that is true to who I am and building a business that is meaningful to me has enriched my life in ways that my six-figure attorney job never could. I love what I do. I am inspired by each and every one of my client's journeys. Seeing my clients fulfil their potential, manifest their dreams and transform their lives is proving to be the greatest gift of all. Absolutely priceless!

Chapter Five

In Your Dreams!

Nothing is impossible. The word itself says *I'm possible*.

—Audrey Hepburn

One of the by-products of redefining my life these last two years is that I've had to step outside my comfort zone. I've learned more in these last couple years than I have my entire life. I am forever grateful to Brené Brown for her TED Talk that prompted me to dare greatly. If I hadn't seen her video, I might not have taken that first step toward building my own coaching business. I no longer doubt my ability to make things happen. I know I am strong enough, brave enough, and resilient enough to live life on my own terms. Will I get it right every single time? Absolutely not. I know that I will make mistakes along the way as I build my business. But I also know that each mistake will help to steer me in the right direction. With each step forward in my business, I know that I am fulfilling my dream of helping as many people as I can to live boldly and without regret.

Sometimes inspiration comes out of the blue. Below are some examples of people who dared greatly. I hope that one of these examples will inspire you to pursue your dreams.

Orville and Wilbur Wright's bicycle retail business helped them to gain the skills necessary to become aviation pioneers. They were able to use what they learned from working on bicycles to successfully build a flying machine.

Until Roger Bannister ran the first sub-four-minute mile (clocking 3:59.4) on May 6, 1954, it was commonly thought to be impossible to run a mile in less than four minutes. After Bannister broke the four-minute mile barrier, 46 days later John Landy, Bannister's rival, clocked a 3:58.0 mile, breaking Bannister's record.

Mark Burnett created the Eco-Challenge, a multi-day expedition-length adventure race, in 1995. Teams of four raced non-stop, 24 hours a day, over a rugged 300-mile course that included such disciplines as orienteering, mountain biking, sea kayaking, mountaineering, rappelling, canyoneering, horseback riding, whitewater canoeing and trekking. The races took place between 1995 and 2002.

Edmund Hillary, who was a New Zealand beekeeper, and Nepalese Sherpa Tenzing Norgay were the first climbers confirmed to have reached the summit of Mount Everest on May 29, 1953.

In 2002, Pam Reed became the first woman to win the Badwater Ultramarathon, a 135-mile footrace through Death Valley. It's billed as the world's toughest footrace. Pam Reed repeated as champion in 2003.

At the 2014 Boston Marathon, runners set out to reclaim the race from the horrors of the terrorist bombings that occurred in 2013. Every person who showed up to race on Monday, April 21, 2014, was there for a greater purpose. Boston Strong! So many inspirational stories! Elite American runner Shalane Flanagan set a blistering pace right off the start line. Although she didn't win the race, she ran with incredible courage, finishing in seventh place as the top-ranked American woman. American Meb Keflezighi's ability to pull out the win over seven other elite male runners who had faster personal bests than he did was a demonstration of grit and determination that brought tears to my eyes (and I'm sure to many others' eyes too).

What all of these people have in common is that they all decided to get up off the couch and acquire the training, skills and resources necessary to accomplish their goals. They pushed beyond what was easy, what was comfortable, to succeed. The Wright brothers didn't just wake up one morning and build a flying machine. Roger Bannister didn't break the four-minute-mile barrier the first time he ran a mile. The teams participating in the Eco-Challenge weren't born skilled in all of the disciplines required to successfully finish the race. Edmund Hillary and Tenzing Norgay honed their climbing skills before attempting Mount Everest. Pam Reed gained endurance and toughness through years of training to win the Badwater Ultramarathon. These are people who had the courage to give the best of themselves to the world, to give the world all that they had to give.

As Eleanor Roosevelt said, "Do one thing every day that scares you." I ask you, would you rather be someone who gives the world the best you've got to give or someone who sits on the sidelines watching the world go by? I implore you to put away all of your doubts: *I'm not talented enough, I'm not brave enough, I'm not special enough …* Yes, you are. I believe there's at least one moment in your life when you showed courage, you figured something out and you exhibited your unique talents. Think back to when you were a kid to the first time you walked to school by yourself or learned to cross the street without holding your mom or your dad's hand. What about your first dance recital or the first time you stepped on the ice and learned to skate? What about the time you auditioned for the school play or for the school choir? I have no doubt that there have been many times in your life when you've displayed courage or shown your unique talents. I invite you to draw on the memories of those successes and how you felt in those moments to help you push past your self-doubt. Ask yourself, *Why not me?*

Chapter Six

Be the Hero of Your Own Story

Never underestimate the power of dreams and the influence of the human spirit. We are all the same on this notion: the potential for greatness lives within each of us.

—Wilma Rudolph

Never in my wildest dreams would I have thought that I would be pressing the reset button on my life at the age of 50. That's the great thing about life: sometimes you just don't know where your journey will take you. I know that I'm not the first person, and I certainly won't be the last, to experience a health crisis, forcing me to reassess my life.

The biggest lesson that I've learned from leaving my cushy job as an attorney is that it's never too late to live authentically with purpose and meaning. I walked away from my job more than two years ago, never to return. Looking back, that was the best move I ever made. For once in my life, I allowed myself to be guided by my heart rather than my head. And that has made all the difference.

I was fortunate enough to be able to hit the reset button at age 50 and to embark on a journey to follow my dreams, my passion, my calling. My work as a coach doesn't feel like work.

CLAIRE YEUNG

I love what I do. I'm excited to give my best every single day. How many people can say that about their jobs?

The journey hasn't been all blue skies and daisies. But the crests and valleys have been worth it. Were there times when I thought that I should just go find another job as an attorney? Absolutely. Did I have to retool and rethink my business along the way? Absolutely. Were there moments when I doubted myself and felt like a failure? Absolutely. Through it all, what kept me going was the knowledge that in order to succeed, I have to allow myself to fail. I've learned from each of my failed attempts and have become much more resilient as a result.

I take great comfort in knowing that giving myself permission to fail is probably the single most important building block toward reaching my goals.

Case in point: James Dyson, the inventor of the revolutionary cyclonic vacuum cleaner. It took 12 years and more than 5,000 iterations for the now iconic cyclonic Dyson vacuum cleaner to come to life. During that time, people told Dyson that if there were such a thing as a better vacuum, Hoover or Electrolux would've invented it. Luckily for us, he didn't listen to the doubters. His perseverance and dogged determination allowed him to learn from each of the 5000-plus iterations until he hit on the final product. Today, Dyson is the world leader, offering the gold standard in vacuum cleaners. As an aside, Dyson also reinvented the electric fan by creating the Air Multiplier. Who would've thought you could make a fan without blades? Dyson made it happen.

There are no guarantees in life. Dyson didn't know for sure that he would invent a revolutionary vacuum. But he had a vision, and he believed in himself enough to bring that vision to life. None of us knows for sure whether our vision will resonate with the rest of the world or whether we will be able to make a difference with an invention. But if we don't put it out there for the world to see and experience, then we pretty much guarantee that we won't make a difference.

In answer to the question, What can't I *not* do in my lifetime? *Live boldly; dare greatly!*

I've told you my story; now it's your turn to become the hero in your own story. The next chapter of this book is full of exercises and tips to help you live boldly and without regret.

Chapter Seven

Your Turn

Your time is limited, so don't waste it living someone else's life. Don't be trapped by dogma—which is living with the results of other people's thinking. Don't let the noise of others' opinions drown out your own inner voice. And most important, have the courage to follow your heart and intuition.

—Steve Jobs

This chapter is all about you. The exercises and tips on the following pages will help you begin your journey to become the hero of your own story. As you go through the exercises, keep these questions in mind:

- How do I want to be remembered?
- What kind of legacy do I want to leave?
- What would I regret not doing in my lifetime?

Worksheet 1
Wheel of Life Self-Assessment

This first exercise will help you to take that first step toward living a more satisfying life. The Wheel of Life represents the different dimensions in your life, with well-being at the centre.

Wheel of Life

1. The first step toward living a more fulfilling life is to figure out how you are feeling about your life right now. Using a scale of one to five, with five being the highest, assess the level of satisfaction you are currently experiencing in each dimension of your life.

Creativity: _____

Fun and Recreation: _____

Career and Business: _____

Personal and Spiritual Growth: _____

Abundance (prosperity, gifts, blessings): _____

Relationships: _____

Community and Social Contribution: _____

Family and Friends: _____

Well-being: _____

2. What would it take to increase your level of satisfaction in each dimension of your life? (It might help you to ask yourself, *If anything were possible, what would I like this area of my life to look like?*) Jot down two or three things that you could change or accomplish in each dimension of your life that would help you be more satisfied.

Creativity:

Fun and Recreation:

Career and Business:

Personal and Spiritual Growth:

Abundance (prosperity, gifts, blessings):

Relationships:

Community and Social Contribution:

Family and Friends:

Well-being:

3. Pick one or two dimensions of your life that you would like to focus on right now. Ask yourself, *What is one thing I can do to get myself closer to being more satisfied in this area of my life?* (Use your answers from question 2 to guide you.)

Worksheet 2
Identifying Your Core Values

On the next page, brainstorm five to ten core values that resonate with you. Don't over-think it. Don't quibble over whether or not something is truly a value. Just write down whatever comes to mind. The purpose of this exercise is to help you illuminate what is important to you.

> **Values** (noun): one's principles or standards; one's judgment of what is valuable or important in life. (*Oxford English Dictionary*)

Here's a random list of values to get your creative juices flowing.

abundance	innovation	justice
belonging	passion	determination
faith	security	collaboration
trust	imagination	excellence
honesty	spirituality	success
dynamism	wisdom	authenticity
equality	respect	loyalty
inspiration	risk	balance
strength	joy	integrity
freedom	commitment	fame
intuition	adventure	love
prosperity	appreciation	decisiveness
challenge	contribution	expertise
stillness	tolerance	variety
harmony	compassion	beauty
philanthropy	community	humour
reliability	productivity	order

What are your core values?

1. Write down five to ten core values that are meaningful to you in the space below. If you come up with more than ten core values, that's okay. Write them all down.

2. Now that you've written down your core values, consider whether you are living each dimension of your life in sync with your core values. If you answer no for any dimension of your life, ask yourself, *What is one thing I can do to help align that dimension of my life with my core values?*

Worksheet 3
Strengths and Resources Exercise

The next step in your journey toward living your richest, most fulfilling life is to take stock of your strengths and resources. Identifying your strengths and the resources available to you will help you to maintain your momentum as you strive to live boldly and without regret.

On the next page, list all of your strengths and any resources you have available to you. I'll get you going with a starter list of strengths and resources:

> adaptable, assertive, authentic, calm, candid, capable, collaborative, courageous, creative, dedicated, diplomatic, dynamic, easygoing, empathetic, energetic, enthusiastic, ethical, financially stable, flexible, happy, honest, humorous, independent, innovative, intelligent, loyal, nurturing, optimistic, organized, patient, poised, practical, pragmatic, problem-solver, reliable, resourceful, responsible, self-confident, self-reliant, sincere, spiritual, spontaneous, strong, supportive, trustworthy, well-connected, wise.

When creating your list, don't over-think it, and don't quibble over whether something is a strength or resource. Just write down whatever comes into your head.

Strengths and Resources List:

Worksheet 4
The Eighty-Year Rule

What would you regret *not* doing in your lifetime? On this page, write down the accomplishments that must occur during your lifetime so that you will consider your life to have been satisfying and well lived, a life of few or no regrets.

Worksheet 5

Your "Why"

On this page, write down the "why" behind the items you listed in Worksheet 4. Take some time to consider why those accomplishments are important to you. Also, consider how they relate to your Wheel of Life self-assessment and your values. Knowing the purpose (the "why") behind what you do will help you maintain your forward momentum.

Worksheet 6

Make a Plan

After you've articulated the purpose behind those accomplishments that must occur during your lifetime for you to feel that your life has been well lived, take a look at the strengths and resources that you identified in Worksheet 3.

Ask yourself what strengths and resources you can draw upon to get yourself one step closer to achieving your accomplishments.

Once you've identified the strengths and resources that you will need, ask yourself, *What is one thing I can do to get myself closer to accomplishing this dream/goal? What is the next thing I can do?* And so on.

Worksheet 7

Take Action

Accomplishing your dreams and goals doesn't stop with making the plan. You have to take action. Here's a sample action plan to help you to stay on track.

Goal/Dream: _____

Done	Due Date	Action Steps	Required Resources

Worksheet 8
Habits and Beliefs

As you embark on the journey to accomplish those dreams and goals that will make your life richer and more fulfilling, you will bump up against habits and beliefs that you have formed over the course of your life. Many of our habits come out of our beliefs. For example, I drink warm water during the day because I believe that it aids digestion. We often don't even notice that we have formed a habit, because it's just part of how we live. For the most part, our habits don't get in the way of our lives until we're forced to change or reassess them.

I'm going to ask you to try to break a habit and see what happens. I'm not asking you to do anything earth shattering. This is about everyday habits, like which way you hang a roll of toilet paper.

- Which way do you normally hang the roll of toilet paper? Do you subscribe to the "over orientation" (away from the wall) or the "under orientation"?

- Why do you subscribe to the "over" or "under" orientation? What's the belief you hold that makes you hang the toilet paper that way?

- Whichever way is your preference, I challenge you to hang the roll of toilet paper the opposite way for a week.

- Were you able to leave the toilet paper hung the "wrong" way for a week? If not, how long did you last? Did the other people in your household change it back?

- While the toilet paper was hung the "wrong" way, what thoughts did you have when you saw it?

Here's what happened in my household: My partner and I subscribe to the "over" orientation for toilet paper because we believe that it's easier to tear off the toilet paper from the roll when it's hung that way. When I told my partner I was going to do this experiment, she said, "Don't you dare. It'll screw up the toilet paper." I switched the orientation of the roll in the guest bathroom on Monday morning after my partner left for work. Every time I looked at the roll, all I could think about was that it was hung the wrong way and that it needed to be corrected. I lasted until noon on that same Monday before I had to switch it back.

What is the point of this challenge? Merely to illustrate how much our beliefs and habits inform how we live our lives. If a habit so seemingly trivial as toilet paper orientation is impossible to break, what about those beliefs and habits that are much more important to us?

Let's try another example.

Which side of the road do you drive on, the left side or the right side? In case you're not sure what I'm talking about, in North America, we drive on the right side of the road; in England they drive on the left side of the road. When you visit a country that drives on the opposite side of the road, do you think they drive on the wrong side of the road? I'm betting more than half of you said yes. How many of you thought, *It's not the wrong side, it's just the other side?* I'm betting not very many of you thought that, unless you've spent an extended period of time in countries that drive on both sides of the road.

Isn't it funny how, for most of us, what we're familiar with, what we're used to, becomes "the right way" and what we're not used to is instantly "the wrong way"? Our beliefs are at the foundation of everything we say and do. Some people won't walk under a ladder because they believe it's bad luck. Some people believe that eating organic produce is healthier and better for the environment. Some of our beliefs are based in science, some are not; some serve us well, some hinder our forward progress. I challenge you to take notice of your beliefs and ask yourself whether they hold you back.

Worksheet 9

Learning to Reframe

When my clients are stuck in "either/or" mode, I ask them to reframe that picture into "both/and." It's a really useful way to get our brains to start thinking in terms of possibilities rather than limits.

In the space below, list the "either/or" notions that are getting in your way and reframe them into "both/and."

Either/Or   **Both/And**

Worksheet 10:

Creative Space

This page is for you to write, draw or scribble in crayon (whichever feels right to you) whatever your heart desires. Allowing your brain to be wildly creative will help you to envision what it looks like to achieve your dreams/goals.

Worksheet 11

Growing Your Courage

In order to accomplish your dreams and your goals, you will need to draw on your courage. The thing with courage is that you have to cultivate and grow it. You have to test the edges of your courage in order to increase your capacity to be brave. I'm not talking about engaging in risky, life-threatening endeavours. I'm talking about simple, everyday courage. I invite you to take me up on my dare.

I dare you to:

- Do something that scares you.
- Learn a new skill.
- Colour outside the lines.
- Laugh out loud.
- Eat a food you've never eaten before.
- Ride the children's carousel.
- Ask for help.
- Take up a new sport.
- Be authentic.
- Walk barefoot in the park.
- Travel to places you've never been before.
- Learn a foreign language.
- Play hopscotch in the park.
- Do what you love.
- Start a conversation with a stranger in a coffee shop.
- Trust in yourself.
- Be true to who you are.
- Live an awesome life.

Worksheet 12

Maintaining the Momentum

On the following pages are some powerful questions to help you maintain your momentum as you strive to live your best life. Believe that you can keep going and that your journey is worth taking. Jot down your thoughts in the space provided as you ponder these questions.

How do you want to be remembered?

What talent do you have that, if shared with the world, will make the world a better place?

What is important to you?

What is one step you can take that will start you on your journey today?

What is one thing you can do to move toward living your best life?

What single brave decision can you make today to maintain the momentum of your journey?

What is one thing you do well? What other things do you do well?

What is one thing your best friend says you do well? What are other things that your friends say you do well?

What would you like to learn and know in your lifetime?

Worksheet 13

Stepping into the Future

I'd like you to refer to the items you listed in Worksheet 4. For each item, visualize what it looks like to have achieved that goal or dream. Use these questions to help you to form a complete picture in your mind's eye of what it looks like when you step into the future.

- Where are you?
- What do you see around you?
- What's the weather like?
- Who is there with you?
- What are you doing?
- What are the other people doing?
- What do you hear the people around you saying?

Once you've formed a complete picture using the above questions, ask this last question: How does it feel?

Worksheet 14
Sure-Fire Formula for Achieving Your Goals

This framework will help you to achieve your goals, both big and small. For starters, you will need to draw on different parts of yourself—what I like to call your "action heroes." Here are the action heroes you'll need to bring to the party:

- Your Visionary: This action hero dreams up the ideas. The Visionary is in charge of imagining, inventing and innovating. This is where the seeds of possibility are planted.

- Your Designer: This action hero designs the plans for the ideas that the Visionary dreams up. The Designer is in charge of analyzing, planning and problem solving. This part of you figures out how to make the seeds of possibility grow.

- Your Achiever: This action hero implements the plans created by the Designer. The Achiever looks after getting things done. Once the seeds of possibility are planted and there's a plan as to how to make those seeds grow, the Achiever takes action to make it happen.

- Your Skeptic: This action hero plays the role of devil's advocate. The Skeptic is the critical thinker who finds the holes in the ideas and the plans, and assesses the risks in order to improve on what the Visionary and the Designer have come up with. This is where quality control happens.

- Your Observer: This action hero plays the role of the reflective thinker. The Observer helps to keep things on track by preventing the ideas from stalling at the visionary, design or critical-thinking stages. The Observer acts as the objective voice of reason.

Now that you've assembled your team of action heroes, here's how the formula works. (There'll be workspace in the pages that follow for you to put this formula to work. I wanted to give you the formula in its entirety first.)

1. Write down the goal that you would like to accomplish. Drawing on your Visionary, describe in as much detail as possible what accomplishing this goal looks like. (For example, if your goal is to run your first 10K race, you might want to describe what it looks like to finish the race: crossing the finish line with your arms raised in victory while friends and family cheer you on.)

2. Channel your Designer and ask, What is one thing I can do to accomplish my goal? What is the next thing I can do to accomplish my goal? Continue on until you have formulated a step-by-step plan. (Using the 10K race as an example, the first step may be to buy a good pair of running shoes; the next step may be to join a running group.)

3. As you formulate the step-by-step plan, bring in the Skeptic to consider the risks that you may need to account for and how you can improve on your plan. (For the 10K race, you might need to consider whether you should consult with your doctor to make sure that running a race will not jeopardize your health.)

4. Once the plan has been created and the risks have been accounted for, it's time to bring in your Achiever and take that first step toward accomplishing your goal. Plans are no good if you don't take action. (For that 10K race, you have to buy those running shoes and get off the couch and run to achieve that goal.)

5. As you move through your step-by-step plan, allow your Observer to check in on your progress along the way. Are you getting hung up on a particular step of the plan? Are you encountering obstacles along the

way? It's up to your Observer to identify what may be preventing you from taking action and to send the plan back to the Designer and the Skeptic to revise and revamp so that your Achiever can get over those speed bumps along the way.

One last thing: remember to believe in yourself! You have an entire team of action heroes behind you!

Step 1: Write down the goal that you would like to accomplish. Drawing on your Visionary, describe in as much detail as possible what accomplishing this goal looks like.

Step 2: Channel your Designer and ask, What is one thing I can do to accomplish my goal? What is the next thing I can do to accomplish my goal? Continue on until you have formulated a step-by-step plan.

Step 3: As you formulate the step-by-step plan, bring in the Skeptic to consider the risks that you may need to account for and identify how you can improve on your plan.

Step 4: Once the plan has been created and the risks have been accounted for, it's time to bring in your Achiever and take that first step toward accomplishing your goal. Plans are no good if you don't take action. Use this space to write, draw or adhere anything that will inspire your Achiever to take action.

Step 5: As you move through your step-by-step plan, allow your Observer to check in on your progress along the way. Are you getting hung up on a particular step of the plan? Are you encountering obstacles along the way? It's up to your Observer to identify what may be preventing you from taking action and then to send the plan back to the Designer and the Skeptic to revise and revamp the plan so that your Achiever can get over those speed bumps along the way. Use this space to record any patterns in your behaviour or any beliefs you may have that are getting in the way of your forward momentum.

Worksheet 15

Celebrate Your Authentic Self

In the space below, describe your authentic self. What does being authentic mean to you? Once you've finished describing your authentic self, take a look at what you've written down and tell yourself that you are awesome! In future, when you experience moments of doubt, come back to this and remind yourself of who you are and what's important to you.

Afterword

Life Lessons from My Grandma

In one of the stars I shall be living. In one of them I shall be laughing. And so it will be as if all the stars were laughing when you look at the sky at night.
— Antoine de Saint-Exupery, *The Little Prince*

During the writing of this book, my grandma Kam Wan Kitty Siu passed away. She was 98 years old. I opened this book with a dedication to my grandpa Henry Hon Lit Siu; it seems fitting that I close this book with a chapter about my grandma.

My grandma was 52 when she gave up her career as a principal of an elementary school in Hong Kong to move to Vancouver, British Columbia. The adjustment from professional career woman to housewife must have been incredibly tough for her, although I never heard her complain about it, not even once. She accepted the move for what it was: a chance to start a new life in a country that wasn't living in the shadow of Communist China. Shortly after we all arrived in Canada, my cousin Caroline was born—the first of the first-generation Canadians in my family. I know that Caroline's birth gave meaning to my grandma's life. Caroline's mom, my aunt Connie, was a young doctor when Caroline was born. My grandma looked after Caroline so that Aunt Connie could continue with her medical career. Such things as maternity leave were unheard of in 1969. A year after Caroline was born, her brother, Ian, came along. My grandma pretty much single-handedly looked after the three of us while we were growing up so that our respective parents could work. Caroline, Ian and I are more like siblings than cousins because we grew up together.

Looking back now, I can fully appreciate what an amazing woman my grandma was. She was strong and courageous and wise beyond words. But she was also incredibly practical and pragmatic. She prepared for every eventuality. She had some crazy habits too, like stockpiling toilet paper (a habit that I've picked up, much to my partner, Vivienne's, chagrin). Most of all, she taught me a lot about how you should conduct and carry yourself in life. Here are some of the life lessons I learned from my grandma.

- Always be humble and understated as you go through life. Flash doesn't matter. It's the substance of who you are that matters. Flamboyance is nothing if you don't have the substance to back it up.

- Girls have to get a good education and have a career. Never depend on someone else to look after you. Stand on your own two feet.

- If you have an important meeting, do not take the elevator to that meeting. Always take the stairs, just in case there's a malfunction with the elevator. You don't want to miss your meeting. Likewise, if you have an exam, you don't want to get stuck in an elevator and miss writing your exam.

- Eat a little of all the foods you like. Don't overeat. But don't deprive yourself either. Balance is the key.

- Don't be disagreeable or difficult. Don't pick fights with other people. But don't be a pushover either. Defend yourself against people who try to hurt or harm you.

- Save your money. Don't spend it on frivolous items. Those items will not provide any benefit to you in the long run, whereas having money in your bank account will afford you independence.

- Do a little exercise so you don't get fat. But don't overdo it, because too much exercise is no good either. (I was never able to follow this piece of advice. I took up marathon running, much to my grandma's horror. But I think she was quite impressed that I could run such long distances without falling over dead.)

- Find a partner who will respect you and be kind to you. (My grandma loved Vivienne to death. They totally bonded from the first day they met. My grandma came to our wedding and was super happy for us when we got married. Pretty cool for an old Chinese woman!)

- Cherish your family. Be good to each other.

- When you're competing against other people in a sport or a game, it's okay to play hard and win. But be gracious in victory. Never rub anyone's nose in the loss.

- Always keep your brain active, and continue learning, no matter how old you are. (My grandma watched *Jeopardy!* and *Wheel of Fortune* to the day she died. She and I used to watch game shows together; I was always amazed at how smart she was and how much knowledge she possessed.)

- It's better to be smart than to be pretty. Don't worry too much about your looks. People won't care what you look like if you show them you are a smart person.

- Work hard. Nothing beats hard work for getting results. There are no shortcuts to success.

- Read books. There is a lot of wisdom to be gained from reading. (My grandma was a voracious reader. She always had a couple of books on the go.)

- Inform yourself of what's going on in the world. It's not good to be ignorant of world events.

I don't think that I would have grown up to be the person I am today without my grandma's influence. Not a day goes by when I don't think about her. I miss her immensely. What I remember most about my grandma is her kind, smiling face. I am incredibly grateful for all of the wisdom that my grandma imparted upon me. I will carry her spirit with me the rest of my days.

Other People's Wisdom

Below are some of my favourite inspirational quotes. These words of wisdom help me to regain my momentum when I get stuck in a rut in my work, my training, my life. Perhaps some of these gems will resonate with you.

"Do or do not. There is no try." Yoda

"You are never too old to set another goal or to dream a new dream." C. S. Lewis

"Shut up, legs!" Jens Voigt

"Winning has nothing to do with racing. Most days don't have races anyway. Winning is about struggle and effort and optimism, and never, ever, ever giving up." Amby Burfoot

"Make sure your worst enemy doesn't live between your own two ears." Laird Hamilton

"If you have the courage to fail, then you have the courage to succeed." Shalane Flanagan

"But I also realize that winning doesn't always mean getting first place; it means getting the best out of myself." Meb Keflezighi

"Be the change you wish to see in the world." Mahatma Gandhi

"Life is like a 10-speed bicycle. Most of us have gears we never use." Charles Schultz

"I would rather have 30 minutes of wonderful than a lifetime of nothing special." Robert Harling

THANK YOU!

To my parents, Eileen and Francis. Your love, support, encouragement and undying belief in me gave me the strength I needed to dare greatly.

To my partner, Vivienne. Your love and support allowed me to transform my life. I couldn't have done it without you. Thanks for coming up with the Eighty-Year Rule!

To my fellow Whole Person Certified Coaches—Janel and Suzanne. You are amazing coaches. Thanks for being in my corner and helping me to see the possibilities.

Open Book Editions
A Berrett-Koehler Partner

Open Book Editions is a joint venture between Berrett-Koehler Publishers and Author Solutions, the market leader in self-publishing. There are many more aspiring authors who share Berrett-Koehler's mission than we can sustainably publish. To serve these authors, Open Book Editions offers a comprehensive self-publishing opportunity.

A Shared Mission

Open Book Editions welcomes authors who share the Berrett-Koehler mission—Creating a World That Works for All. We believe that to truly create a better world, action is needed at all levels—individual, organizational, and societal. At the individual level, our publications help people align their lives with their values and with their aspirations for a better world. At the organizational level, we promote progressive leadership and management practices, socially responsible approaches to business, and humane and effective organizations. At the societal level, we publish content that advances social and economic justice, shared prosperity, sustainability, and new solutions to national and global issues.

Open Book Editions represents a new way to further the BK mission and expand our community. We look forward to helping more authors challenge conventional thinking, introduce new ideas, and foster positive change.

For more information, see the Open Book Editions website:
http://www.iuniverse.com/Packages/OpenBookEditions.aspx

Join the BK Community! See exclusive author videos, join discussion groups, find out about upcoming events, read author blogs, and much more! http://bkcommunity.com/